For Julian

ACKNOWLEDGEMENTS

Acknowledgements are due to the editors of the following publications in which versions of these poems first appeared: *Being Alive* (Bloodaxe Books, 2004), *Boomerang, The Manhattan Review, Poetry London, Poetry Review, The Rialto*, and the British Council *First Lines* website.

'The Voyage of the Rays' was first broadcast on BBC Radio 4 as part of the National Poetry Day celebrations in 2001 and 'Baize' was commissioned and broadcast by BBC Radio 3 in 2002. 'Women' won first prize in the *Mslexia* poetry competition 2004 and 'Buffalo Mozzarella' won first prize in the same competition in 2005. 'Dumbarton' was a prizewinner in the Bridport poetry competition in 2004.

I am grateful to the Jerwood Foundation and Cove Park, the artists' residency centre in Scotland, for a grant in 2001 which gave me time and space to write. In 2003 I received a grant from Arts Council England South East which helped enormously in giving me time to work on this book.

Thanks are due to Esther Morgan, Jane Griffiths, and especially to Joanne Limburg for their painstaking reading of many of these poems and their advice which definitely made them better. Thanks also to Matthew Hollis for his care and expert eye. I am very grateful to Yang Lian for his permission to use my translation of his poem 'Where the River Turns'. Yang Lian is the author of several books in English translation, most recently *Concentric Circles* (Bloodaxe Books, 2005).

CONTENTS

III

I

The Poetry God

has golden hair,
wears a golden ring.

He carries a red valise
in which two pairs of shoes

walk the inner edge.
He likes *things*.

The Poetry God says
Do you want to be here or not?

If you fear you are alone
a poem is a kind of love.

We lie down together
in a faded room.

We get on with the business
of filling the empty page.

My Life, the Sea

There was a time when I was empty
and my life was ravenous: it lapped at me
though I had nothing to give it.
It yowled in the rolling rooms I inhabited,
it pawed the lovers who followed me there
to see what they were made of, recoiling
when it found them full of gold and blood.
I was weak and I lied to my life.
It sobbed at the shore as I left, its face ugly,
its breath sour. It swore to drink itself to death.
I opened my mouth to the sky and the sun.
I was free as a ghost. I stopped speaking.
I hid myself in crowds and a new language.
Sometimes phones would ring when I passed them.
Sometimes letters would reach me, torn into pieces.
I never spoke of my life and it did not find me,
except at night when I rolled wide awake
and it slept in my arms like a beautiful fish.

The Voyage of the Rays

Skirts fluttering,
they melt through the water,
rippling the sleep of the boat.

Each gasps a satisfaction
at the haul from sea into fire,
the flash of hands,

the scorch of the floor.
Each beats her tail feebly, rolls the sun
over the gloss of her spine,

her bleeding lip pressed
against a window of wood.
Her message is her body

winded at his feet,
eyes sinking in relief
at the journey completed.

He throws each back,
watches her turn, a medal in space,
but still they keep coming,

surfacing like dreams he has no answer to,
filling all the ocean
with trembling politeness.

Swan

I thought that it was you
turning to me for an instant
from the blindness of the water,

a pure white question,
with its underwater dream in tow
softening the stones at my feet.

I thought that it was you
and if not you, then love itself
tacking perfectly towards me,

rocking in its own beauty,
the circles backing out
like people not quite believing.

Fishing Boat

I wanted so much to save it,
the carved sea, the white sky
bleaching me away.

The peregrines whipped from the chalk,
rushed up the cliff-face
like ash from the baking sea,

and I wanted so much to save it,
how we lay down, and the sun
fired our shadows into the rock.

Far below a fishing boat chugged
like a toy, pushing its blue V
to somewhere familiar,

and I saw the skipper recording,
I saw that he would be the one
to draft the flutter of clothes,

the obliteration of skin by sun,
the *are they…? are they…?*
as the boat led him out of sight

of the dust and pebbles kicked
slowly down the chalky face.
I saw him scribbling the whispers,

the madness, the too-little time,
as the boat and its trawl of glimpses
slipped away from me, towards home.

Hedgehog

Its leg was not broken. It was not homeless.
It clenched in my hands, a living flinch.
You cannot love so much and live,
it whispered, its spines clicking like teeth.
I hid it from itself in a cardboard box.

Overnight it nibbled a hole and slipped away.
I cried so much my mother thought I'd never stop.
She said, *you cannot love so* – and yet
I grew to average size and amused a lot of people
with my prickliness and brilliant escapes.

Elvis the Performing Octopus

hangs in the tank like a ruined balloon,
an eight-armed suit sucked empty,

ushering the briefest whisper
across the surface, keeping

his slurred drift steady with an effort
massive as the ocean resisting the moon.

When the last technician,
whistling his own colourless tune,

splashes through the disinfectant tray,
one might see, had anyone been left to look,

Elvis changing from spilt milk to tumbling blue,
pulsing with colour like a forest in sunlight.

Elvis does the full range, even the spinning top
that never quite worked out, as the striplight fizzes

and the flylamp cracks like a firework.
Elvis has the water applauding,

and the brooms, the draped cloths, the dripping tap,
might say that a story that ends in the wrong place

always ends like this –
fabulous in an empty room,

unravelled by the tender men in white,
laid out softly in the morning.

Nibbling

Devastated cobwebs
cling to her lashes. She's

a crazed dictator, disappearing
whole families of scorching pink.

The pin faces of forget-me-nots
giggle as she opens wide.

She rips the hearts out of dandelions
and snaps the backs of mint in two.

In dreams I take her with me,
tightly in my arms,

and I set her gently down
wherever lawns have lost their mind.

Buffalo Mozzarella

When I say that I tasted him
I mean that I knew the stale
baby-press of his mouth,
his cold breath, and the way
he scratched the cushion of his thumb
on his stubbled cheek. See –

how he leans in the litter bin,
his arm digging deep,
to feel among the cut of beer cans
the abominable plastic, the rub of old fat,
as if there should be flesh there,
something gentle to welcome him.

And then he finds it – the sundried tomato
and buffalo mozzarella sandwich
I had just one bite out of because I saw
the one thing that scared me most,
and I dropped my sandwich with its one
shell-shaped ticklishly damp bite out.

I didn't think that a mouth
more silent than mine
would nuzzle where my lips had been
and bite out a shape to caress mine,
nibbling, delicate, not rushing at all –
and that someone else's hunger

and sorrow and spit would devour mine.
When I say that I tasted him
I mean that the night shook me awake
and I saw the back of his head clearly
as he bent down into darkness and shame
to find out the truth about me.

Naked

I'm just knotting my tie
nice and tight for the presentation
when out of the corner of my eye
I see my wife, looking a bit cold

with a tray in her hands, and two glasses.
I'm your naked waitress
she says, staring at me from the door –
Derek, can you believe it? –

and I smile and steer her into bed
and down the champagne and say *later*
you crazy thing and tuck her in
and get out just in time, and I mean *just*

for the 8.30 to Euston where I'm opposite
this girl, late teens, not-reading
Cosmopolitan and staring out
at the fields breaking into grey.

I'm going to meet my father, she says
for the very first time. Derek, the world's
gone mad, I nearly scream. Why can't people
just say normal things, be normal?

But my new watch tells me that at least
I'm still on track for the presentation
and when the train pulls in I say,
'Let me carry that for you,' and up we go.

'Good luck!' I hoot, and I'm off,
top speed, Derek, and on the tube,
you can't blame me, I'm imagining her naked,
but the pictures get mixed up and ruin it all,

because she's smiling, even in my head,
as if she's having all her birthdays at once
as if that station is her all-time favourite place,
as if having no kit on doesn't matter a bit.

In Scunthorpe

Conforming, I walk the corporation
knit of streets, the park patio-flat,
the snow a rumpled doily on the arm
stumps of walls. The air is slate-cold

and on the road in, the steel works
wear a drunk uncle hat for Christmas.
This road is the mutest in England,
and a woman can almost lose herself

in the naked trees. Hungry for romance
I roll the snowman's beer and chips belly
carefully through ice till we stop.
He leers at me in his too-big cap

and wakes grinning, etched with soot.
The name has buried itself in us,
the road out is sniggers and whispers.
We don't say a word. We speed up.

Oxford Bus

First we passed the shops, hot and open,
pleading with us to stop. I saw the dresses
wave, their hats bowed, their shoes crossed.

On the High we rode the shoulders of the lost,
the woman with the teddy bear and the dots of rouge
cried out to someone, but we were gone,

and the creature in his twisted baseball cap
stopped singing and pulled in to let us pass,
because we had a known destination,

and you have to bow to those strong enough
to leave themselves behind. I'm that sort of course,
and so when we passed her I didn't stare for long

at the face that was clearly mine, accusing me
from a rippling window, clinging to the seat in front
and crying *How did I get here? Where can I go?*

Nagyvázsony Castle

Balaton, Hungary

There was a time when I was buried
deep in the walls of a far ruin

and it was not language that saved me,
nor was it history, nor was it me at all,

but the way that certain people can sense
warmth through stone and start pulling.

Far below, my friends are laughing,
children squeal to the stocks and the dungeon.

The green country I remember reaches out,
sunflowers break its heart, vines stitch it whole.

I remember the incantation,
the laying on of hands,

my blanket as I got to my feet,
the command to be forever amazed.

Sindy and Me

While Sindy, dressed in sparkly pink,
drifted around her plastic apartment,

I dreamed of a far blue-green planet,
like earth, round which I drifted

softly on a weightless rope.
I made the planet smaller and more silent

by dreaming the rope longer,
my tumbling amniotic and delicious.

Sindy sat mounted on her orange horse
and surveyed the carpet's far swirling.

I found that dreaming the rope longer
was no longer enough:

I still could hear the rattle of snakes,
the hiss of clouds, the arguments of sharks.

Sindy stood unmoved in her plastic kitchen.
Her green rubber knife posed no real threat.

I took out my knife, and cut the cord.
I did not weep at all, I found that sleep

is exactly the mathematical shape of space
funnelling out beyond sisters and dust.

Baize

I should have tried harder
to love Steve Davis.
If not for his neat bow tie
then for his rare motor skills.

Good hand-eye co-ordination
smooths the path of a relationship.
At least one of you must have it,
like hope, and the ability

to love and keep one's word.
There was much I failed to understand
that Steve tried to explain:
that life's a process of elimination,

and the black truth must be toyed with
until it's the only way out.
One must maximise one's options
within the frame the game creates,

avoiding conflict until its result
can be decisive in your favour –
and the one true art is procrastination
so complex it appears something is happening

until finally, the smack of the cue
drives uncertainty off the face of the earth.
I've learned at last I don't need anything
that requires a hand to touch me.

I dream of the long green baize
where Steve and I might have lain,
my unmanageable dreams
finally, gratefully, pocketed.

The Lexicographer Finishes P

There's going to be a party when they finish P,
he says. He's only a part-time lexicographer,
at heart he is a poet. I sip
and wonder how he can resist escape
from the palace which is really a prison
into the secret tunnel of O or the labyrinth of Q.
He's a palimpsest: in his hands are the shadows
of F and faint etching of K, and one deep swirl of C.
With such ease he's abandoned one letter for another,
in love with the primitive after enjoying the modern,
a pantheist who no longer answers to God.
I want to tell him,
take me with you.
I'm passionate enough for P,
I get palpitations when I think of perfection;
I believe in paradise, I believe in the permanent,
(and in possibilities), today I'm a pasque-flower,
tomorrow a paramour. I can learn to keep my peace.
There is a pause.
He's perturbed, pouting, pushing away his cappuccino.
I've even changed my name, I say. *Please.*

II

Dumbarton

In changing my life I got as far as Dumbarton.
It was midnight. She didn't believe I loved her,
so I rang her and said, *I'm getting in the car now*
and I found myself swallowing the road out of Glasgow,
the bridge screaming at me to leave then, leave.

I rang her. I hated my voice. *I'm so tired
darling, tired*, I said. The click told me
that the future is as uncertain as the past.
The road was empty, my whole body ached.
I had nine points on my licence and so

had to crawl my way to my brand new life.
She didn't believe I loved her. I rang her.
I've left everything for you, I said. Or,
You're everything to me. Or perhaps
I said nothing at all, being smashed

upside-down in the central reservation.
The lights of Dumbarton were mostly out
as I turned back. The stars were gibberish,
the road flat on its back. I rang her. I hated my voice.
I'm so tired, darling, tired. Forgive me.

Proposal from the Bottle Bank

I am taking the empties to the bottle bank.
The car clinks like a nervous ice cream van.
When I open the boot, the green wine-eyes wink.

I lay the crates in the mud of footprints.
My face is wet. When I lick my fingers I taste you.
I sweat like the hot hours before a hangover.

The first bottle breaks and I imagine your dress
around your waist, your face turned away.
You are cool against me. You are *whiteness*.

The hole of the bank is rusted and hungry.
Like your mouth it takes whatever I give it.
The smell of wine, sharp as grief, swallows me.

They fall one by one into the dark.
Will you love this? Forever? I ask,
in the swirling rain, multicoloured as trash.

My Husband

lives by the sea.
His windows shudder in sea storms.
The gun-blue clouds drift

across the waves like airships.
My husband has a red wine stain
across his expensive white carpet.

I knocked over my glass
the first time I went there.
I didn't mention the husband-thing.

I think of my husband
as the city whispers
like a hungry, birdless ocean.

I keep the phone close
in case he should decide
to come and save his wife.

Your Wife

I think of your wife.
She is real and warm
as a cat in my arms.

She smiles at the top of a staircase.
She dreams like a cat,
a murmur that wakes no one.

When I think of your wife
you are leaving her.
She glances up at the first word.

And afterwards
someone leads her
to the edge of a bright ocean.

She cannot escape it
though she writes herself a raft
and clambers on it.

I send her a message in a bottle.
She lifts her head in the sun.
Will she open it?

Her hair is plastered to her face.
But she knows you.
She unwraps my message,

finds a poem that she scans
a thousand times.
I think of your wife

as you lay me
beneath you
and what I feel

when your hands are on me
is no pain
and white peace

like a sky filling everything.
I think of nothing.
Nothing I want is shocking.

Mule

He snaps five halters before I learn
that four hooves dug in means *no*.
I try weeping. I try weaving

a trail of Polos down the yard.
I tickle him under the chin.
He regards me without amusement.

I think he loves me, even as he sinks
his long teeth into my head when I drag
his foreleg an inch. I cry at his feet.

I nibble hay and try to understand.
I gather the Polos and feed them to him.
His lips are wet and grateful.

This is the language of refusal,
the eternal tenderness
of things that will not move.

By sunrise, he is my creature
and this is my home.
I cry and I beat him. I do not leave.

Women

I sail into the world of women,
in a magnificent ship that does not interest them.

I imagine this is what loving them is:
adding up the piecework of them,

the pale neck, the sudden crow's feet,
the expensive lips saying *of course of course.*

I have learned their language, I can say
what do you think? like a native,

but they detect an accent in spite of me.
Their eyes rest on me over the wine.

Their secrets are palpable as money.
We trade, and I grow rich. I feel free.

We compare songs, the cuts on our wrists.
Sometimes I think I have found my home.

When I hold them, I hear their bones crying.
Their costly hair drifts and shines.

Two Views of Loch Long

I *Dance*

In the evening when the loch
ruffles like a skirt made of steel
my father comes back from the dead
to show me his latest steps.

He loved to dance; he danced until
he could no longer hold the women to him,
until he fell down in the street, got back up,
each step an awkward new-learned move.

But not tonight. Tonight he holds me
and I feel his warmth against my face.
He says (everything the dead say is new)
Close your eyes. Remember me.

I go back into the kitchen, say hello
to someone, put on the radio.
His warmth haunts my hands for hours.
I touch a cup. The world moves.

I search my thoughts of you.
I want to say, *Here is the reason*

you should be with me. I have found it.
I keep everything, from kissed matchboxes

to guides to Shanklin Chine.
That poet's sweater for example:

I made him give it to me and I wore it everywhere
though people laughed at the way it dwarfed me.

This item will explain it all.
We made it. It is smooth and deep.

We made it, together in the dark
like a careful surgeon and a clever tailor

who discover one night they are one and the same.
I have searched for days. I have not slept.

I would know it anywhere.
Its moon is missing.

Do you remember? At night
its waters fill with moving light,

like the first wheel ever made
each spoke perfect and on fire.

Two Views of a Submarine

Loch Long

I

The loch is a factory where darkness
is welded and sparked into life,

sent up to breathe like a whale,
the water shattering from its back.

Ferries cross in shiny home-comings,
the loch trembles with a soft pulse

and an echo is sent to live in my skin.
It is a call to witness a miracle:

my wish in its flat black hat
ballooning out of the waves.

II

When I imagined exactly this
tilt and drift into the dark

I thought I would go mad for you,
that I would forgive everything.

But as I slowly press these walls
like Alice in her Wonderland

who was a child, and simply
reached for whatever caught her eye

and then suddenly did not fit her life,
I know that I would give you up

instantly for oxygen, or hope.
My murmured bargain creaks:

it is being considered, deeply.
I close my eyes and my wish

is granted: I wake open-mouthed,
drenched, cold, in flickering air.

Still Life with Table and Loch

Kilcreggan, Scotland

The long gleam with dead flowers,
the china bowl of small essentials.

The clutter of objects, domestic or hopeful,
the mug of wine with its grubby sheep,

and at the edge a woman asleep,
a woman who still calls herself a girl,

desperate as she is for submarines to turn
to doves or secret monsters.

The birdbath is empty but eager,
its plain face damp with imaginings,

but the horizon is not sentimental:
once again, it explains the violet islands.

The loch is posing for itself today,
starlet-blue, its mermaid tail out to sea.

Its waters are dimpled and young.
It remembers very little today.

Wave

A low, restless shore,
and a high sun,
sharp as the blade-red
of the oystercatchers
hustling the old sea.

It was just a walk:
no thought to think through,
no fear to work through,
my shadow inconsequential,
my step too light

to dislodge the periwinkles
sucking hard on the rocks,
a grubby, rough population
with its head down. So why
at every step behind me,

did the rockpools clink
and the shingle tock-tick
as the shells let slip and rolled?
I stopped, checked the sun,
jostled my shadow.

It raised itself, my lazy chill,
and the periwinkles fell
with a blaze of shell-shine
into the wave my dark arm
promised but did not bring.

There was no anger at God
for not delivering the sea.
Just the sighs of the tiny
and upside-down, resigned
to the never-rock, the un-brine.

Fairytale

I search for our story;
my footprints follow
unthinkingly, an untidy line.

A kingfisher sparks
and flickers ahead of me
and of course I follow it

though it leads me only
to where the ducks in formation
know the secret of what comes next.

They drag their perfect lines
until they make sense,
title them with circles,

and send me a rowing boat
with a cargo of voices
and a splash as sharp as a photograph.

I search for our story
down the darkening path
and all that follows

brings me back to this:
to the water, the bridge
and the impossible task,

and the kingfisher's break
from an opening line
bright like a flash of the last.

Defenestration

You with that gentle look,
she trusts you, and trust is essential

when you're going in for the push.
Which window should it be?

Top of the Pécs TV Tower?
The Eiffel? You there, at the end –

what are you waving about? Tell her what?
That *nothing changes* if she goes or stays,

but there's a way to stop the pain
and you're a helping hand?

Brilliant! Give that man a drink!
I love the elegance of the agreed demise.

Now you know the drill: a quick press
to the heart and a swift turnaround –

no one likes to be observed
when they're losing their grip.

And choose a cold day, a flooded day,
with no sunlight and no people,

a day when even you'd believe
there's just no point in going on.

Desiderata

Believe your eyes. When he crumples
it is because a memory has woken

and knocked his legs from under him.
Be always kind: hold out your arms

and find a way not to speak. Silence
is much more valuable than words.

Remember we are all wounded. Try
to see his suffering without panic

that it will crawl from him to you,
and block out all the light in the sky.

It may do this, but it does not mean to.
It is the nature of pain to eat everything.

Forgive all that will be done to you.
Extend your definition to include now.

Believe in everything, time after time.
Dream of caution. Never be yourself.

Domestic Science

My attempts to boil you
out of him failed:
you rose to the surface

like foam in a whiskey vat,
and he gulped you back down
faster than I could scrape you off.

I spent months hoovering
the flakes of you off him.
He didn't thank me for it.

He searched the rubbish
to replace the dust in his hair.
He screamed when I tried

to remove your jagged face
from his chest. He wept.
Our life was a bloody mess:

filleting you out was our only hope.
His pain rang like breaking glass.
My tears made no difference.

He stopped mentioning you at all.
We talked of the place that lies
beyond all this. He cooked supper

and opened a nice bottle of wine
while I laid everything in a circle
to make sure we got there.

Rainbow

We push a trolley through Kitchens
filled with bright things on which we agree.
We buy candles, a water jug, and (nearly)

a cutlery set. Not a life yet but nearly,
bringing home the giddy truth:
a new beginning. We've been so clumsy

but see how the plates shine unbroken?
We shake our heads at Curtains and Lighting
press on through Office Organisation,

just sure enough of what we have
not to ask for too much, yet. We touch down
in Bedrooms, with time arching over us

and our bodies restless. Which frame
will frame us best? Which keep us safe?
Outside the road is pouring with rain,

unbroken for days, but the car starts first time
and we're on our way home, blinking through water,
our treasures clinking in their muddy chest.

XX

They met in Rome, above the ruins of the Forum. Yours was on her first trip in a brand new life of sobriety, and mine had wandered off from his wife and children, and found himself in a new country. They stood next to each other amazed at the jumble laid out before them, and at exactly the same moment each raised a cigarette to their lips. 'Looks like all my coincidences,' he remarked and she, without turning to look, said, 'It looks like my life,' which was clever, but rather serious, and he thought he might cry. For no reason she could think of, she decided to say you were dead, and strangely she felt free now, was that a terrible thing to say? He said he understood completely, some things only end when a person dies. He almost said, *Do you ever think your life would make more sense without you in it?* but by then it was mid-afternoon and the sun was crawling in the ruins, so they agreed to meet later when the day had cooled to tell each other swashbuckling stories about fate and chance, whose endings you and I dream of, and whose beginnings – in the end – no longer feature us.

My America

4th July 2004

Afterwards, I set sail for you.
I hear that no matter

how I lay myself,
tight and frightened

or clean and full of forgiveness,
there's room to start again.

I know life will be hard,
carved from first principles,

there are enemies to crush
with everything we've got.

There are skies to scrape
and a past to speed from

till it's a tiny grey island
that no one remembers.

I land exhausted, with only
a suitcase, broken open,

and at your feet I begin
my book of declarations

that will be our history,
that will make us brand new people.

Beijing

At night the city exhales,
a beast of neon and fog.

By day it grows and forgets,
tiny people pick across

its shoulders, nipples and teeth.
Hundreds fall off each day

in an act of cheap forgetting.
We travel the scars of its skin

towards a sky scraped through
to the blue. My eyes a crane,

I lift faces, swing them back
and forth. I feel I know them,

their machine-blankness,
the factory of their speech.

Far above me, builders clink,
sharp against the sun as children.

This is the making, making,
that our bodies are slave to,

forgetful of losses, of blood,
of ancient, useless, waves of love.

Cheng Du Massage

I lie tidy as an English village
while her fingers sting me with sleet,
her snowball fists smash into me.
She pads around me, light as a coot,
before hammering exploding nails
into my thighs – then on to my temples,
pressing till my eyes spark –
and I see nothing but China's
electric bones, its face of fog –
and my own giant muteness, piled and blind,
unlovely and stubborn as cement.

Flights Over Siberia

And then we tip, with giddy slowness,
like an ice cube or a smooth green olive
drifting through a long, clear gin.
When I see you again we will each have shed
half a world, and ourselves as we go,
as if we were dying forever at high speed.
Below lies the skeletal desert, its spine of ash,
its hide crusted and still, the last thing I see
before I close the blind and turn to sleep.
We each have seen the same forbidden blue,
the same fire too bright to believe, and it is this
that means we hold each other after the fall
of five thousand miles, and know we are alive.

Bride

To be owned is to be the chosen sort,
in the right place at the right time,
with the right plans in the right order.
Today the book falls open at the right page,
the light, though wrong for winter, is right,
my body and my thoughts feel right:
my head, for once, is screwed on right.
I was a child. I peered at life, in awe
of its wrong heart, its right words, its ruthless correctness.
I shut it out. I longed for it. It embarrassed me.
This is what it is to be owned:
I leave the shore where I paced my life.
My pleas for the waves to part, or stop,
are swallowed by the gulls who have forgotten me.
There's a raft now, and every time I add a rock
to my strange map, there is a hand on mine.

III

This translation arises out of my keen interest in, and sympathy for, the themes of exile, isolation and strangeness in the work of Chinese dissident poet Yang Lian. In 2004 I was awarded a residency at Cove Park artists' centre to work with Yang Lian on translating this poem, using a method based on detailed discussion between the two of us about all aspects of the poem, taking place over several days. We used dictionaries and a French translation when we hit an impasse, and most of all we relied upon our close artistic understanding and our mutual desire to render a piece of work that was a poet's translation, not a linguist's. This is the first translation into English of Yang Lian's poem.

Where the River Turns

by YANG LIAN

I

here   a form opens on the sheen of the water
two oily blue wings   fanning out
an autumn that never truly reaches you

an autumn that is here forever   where the river turns
the season again becomes part of you
your eyes   abandoned by all they see

no single thing lasts for long   a bench
sinks deep into its own nature   lost in thinking
the river is carved with tiny cliffs against the light
the ripples splinter like porcelain
and grow together again   the reeds' candle-hearts are a
            shadow-pattern
thrown against the bank   and the bank   drifts out from your heart

the sky's fresh scent excites the dead
as if answering to a conductor's cold and beautiful gesture

II

here   water spreads from two directions   two flashbacks
where the river turns   a man turns away from the passage of time

and the names dug into the bench's back become his
sunlight turns away from the afternoon's dazzling geography

the warmths of other bodies which sat here remember you
the stains of dried-out waters record the dusk

spewed-out   bloodied
the shuttered eye of a crow stares into this moment   from two deaths

the arms of women in a rowing boat drive toward two finishes
swans forced by invisible hunger

slip in beside the river's scented flesh   you exist at the point of
      a fish bone
the pasts in two directions are both empty

III

here   a bird hunted down a marsh
for a grave   its skull snow white and exquisite
like a thought that has given up flying
the day let you sink below its surface
the sweet sound of water immersed you to your brow
hearing became a cave
the river opened a silk screen
the body that spooned the sky now changes at the speed of light
wetness becomes part of you again   but it is a stranger to water
a wet window sieved from the bottom of the river   the wild bush
sucks the beating heart and empty eye socket away

the sky's blue violence like a skullcap placed down

the distant place that can never be reached
forever advances through wings and feet
death is sealed in a crystal box on the bookshelf
the far waterfall hooks you back into air

IV

here   the river turns   the ice-pink bush turns
hear the reed cutter   cutting back what is not dark enough
stars turn to the side we cannot see
all of them in human shape

compound eyes reproduce across the sky
the vast expanse of city lights   surfaces from deep inside your body
cracks criss-cross the water as if from an origin

that has just been rewritten for you
the one you cannot help but accept

                              this swarming rain
that can never reach a real night
is forever the most terrified species

the horizon turns away   you have endless blank waters

the water waves like a drowned hand

stillness becomes part of your skin again   the pearl light is full
          of the river
it gives you *here*   pours to the brim the countless *wheres*
it gives drunkenness a form   on the hill in the darkness
it wears a golden mask   seagulls mirror the invisible sea
like broken white crosses   nailed above your head

                         a drop of rain stings the universe
wash   this pair of ears, torn off and deaf
bear your burden   this transgressed boundary of flesh